# CRY FOR SUDAN

# CRY FOR SUDAN

William Mather

Terra Nova Publications

Published in Great Britain by
Terra Nova Publications
PO Box 2400, Bradford on Avon, Wiltshire BA15 2YN

Illustrations by the author from sketches done on site.
Cover design by Roger Judd, using a sketch by the author
of open air worship in Kajo-Keji, southern Sudan.

Back cover photograph by Martin Cavender
(the author sketching in Naivasha, Kenya).

ISBN  1 90194 933 8

Printed in Great Britain
by Bookmarque Ltd, Croydon

# Contents

Booking Ref: 12355161
Beyonce
20-February-2014        6:30 pm
11727823                Beyonce.com
STANDING                A4353
£60.00                  ADU
07-January-2014
14/11/11/01.01.01.01/01.01.01.01/S10

SECC - The SSE Hydro

The SSE Hydro, Exhibition Way, Glasgow

The Mrs. Carter Show World Tour 2014

Presented by DF Concerts & SJM Concerts

Over 14s in the Standing

**BEYONCÉ**

Level        Door        Block
0            D           STANDING

0                        Ticket No

                         4353

Thursday
20-February-2014
Doors: 6:30 pm        £60.00        Adult

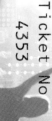

THE SSE HYDRO

Register now at
ticketSOUP.com®
and be amongst
the first to know
about forthcoming
events, special
offers & pre-sales.

**TICKET SOUP**
.COM

MIX
Paper
FSC FSC® C107726

HA/0149761

## CLYDE BUILT.

**BAR & KITCHEN**

**BUILT FOR GREAT EVENTS**

clydebuiltbarandkitchen.co.uk

SECC | 0141 576 3227 |

**TICKETSOUP**.COM

recycle

STAR SECURE TICKETS from AUTHORISED RETAILERS

HA/0149761

## Much More Than A Book

Much more than
Just a book
About the Sudan
But a volume
That speaks to the soul
About ministry
And mission
A meditation
From the heart
That calls to prayer
And seeing the unseen
Helps others to
Understand and experience
A different way
Of thinking
That challenges
Presuppositions
About how we live
And die
And have our being

# Foreword

Like many who grew up in a Christian family, some of whose relatives had 'gone into the mission field', I was used to missionaries coming home and giving illustrated talks about what they did. Like many, I had no idea what on earth they were talking about. Now I realise some of the pain they went through, trying to communicate something vital with those who wanted to know, but who had nothing in their own experience to link it with.

It was only when I went to Africa for the first time, in 1985, on sabbatical leave from the parish where I worked, that I began to understand. I had the privilege of being in Tanzania and Kenya for seven weeks, doing virtually nothing! So I was able to take in the atmosphere, the space, the crowds of people walking, the heat, the hopes and fears, the fragility of life and the depth of the faith that enabled so many to cope.

How do you capture, and communicate, an experience of such intensity that in two weeks your life can be changed?

This is a question that all *SOMA* short-term mission team members face when they return home —and sometimes it is so difficult they give up trying.

The difficulty is even greater when the mission has been to countries where there is acute trauma (as in Rwanda), or long-standing conflict (as in Sudan). Meeting people who have never known life without war – who have seen and experienced things that are so painful they cannot speak about them – makes us feel totally inadequate, and often reduces us to tears.

When *SOMA* first started working in Sudan, we began to realise that the exile (physical for some, emotional for all) had a parallel in the total loss experienced by the children of Israel when, after the capture of Jerusalem, they were taken into exile in Babylon. It was, to say the least, traumatic —and it was a while before at least some could believe that God had not abandoned them. Indeed, it was in Babylon that they began to realise that God was speaking to them in a new way —through poetry, prophecy, and a deeper level of prayer than they had ever experienced before.

The Sudanese we have met need to find a way of speaking about the unspeakable. They have found this through writing their own songs, poetry and laments —and being able to tell God how they feel, without fear of rejection.

This is where this book of drawings and poems comes in. William has the remarkable gift of evoking an atmosphere that normal words cannot convey. For those who have shared the experience with him, or been on similar visits, they bring back memories in a unique and powerful way. My belief and hope is that they will also help those who have never had this privilege, to identify to some degree with what our brothers and sisters in Sudan are still going through.

*Don Brewin*

September 2004

# What is *SOMA*?

*SOMA* stands for 'Sharing of Ministries Abroad' and has just celebrated twenty five years of Christian ministry. Its particular focus is 'Working for the transformation of individuals and churches and the healing of communities and their lands through the renewing power of the Holy Spirit'. As well as organising occasional large conferences its main way of achieving this vision is by sending and receiving teams worldwide on short-term mission within the Anglican Communion. Work with other denominational bodies is also welcomed.

The team visits to the Sudan mentioned in this book have all been part of this. In addition, *SOMA* has been able to create many opportunities for visits to the UK by Sudanese clergy and leaders. Many churches have been blessed as a result.

In the summer of 2004, *SOMA* organised a Silver Jubilee Conference at Canterbury with four hundred guests from around the world. It became very clear that modern mission is increasingly 'from everywhere to everywhere'. Part of this involved inviting about eighty overseas clergy to UK parishes, sharing their insights and experiences of renewal. Even more would have come had their visa applications not been refused.

From its birth in 1978, *SOMA* has spread around the world, with eleven countries now sending out teams. Somewhere between forty and fifty countries have received teams. The teams always go at the invitation of the local bishop, who will often ask them to give teaching on a particular theme. The teams normally comprise up to six people and go on average for ten to fourteen days. An exception to this was the *SOMA* mission to the whole country of Kenya in 2004, with a team of fifty six, who were then joined by a further fifty Kenyans. This very large group then split into smaller teams who fanned out to almost every diocese in the country. Increasingly, such teams are cross-cultural, often made up of people from very different countries and backgrounds.

Many workbooks have been created by Don Brewin, National Director of *SOMA* UK, to provide teaching for teams to take with them. These include topics such as: Renewal for Life; Healing and Wholeness; The Person of Christ; The Work of the Holy Spirit; Discerning the Spirit in the Midst of Chaos; Sharing Your Faith; Marriage; Leadership and Aids.

*SOMA* was born out of a prophetic vision given in Canterbury Cathedral, while a number of bishops were dancing in the Spirit at the east end, during the 1978 *SOMA* conference, just before the Lambeth Conference of bishops from around the world. The vision was to create an organisation to be caring for the nervous system of the church.

In its Mission Statement, *SOMA* describes itself as a 'pilgrim people who stand in our relationship with God, Father, Son and Holy Spirit and under the authority of Holy Scripture'. The work relies heavily on networks of trusting relationships.

On the financial front *SOMA* survives thanks to those who give and pray so generously. Its only source of income is charitable giving from individuals and churches. All *SOMA*'s profits and royalties from sales of this book, for instance, will go to further the work of *SOMA* and *SOMA*-related work in the Sudan. Your interest is deeply appreciated.

If you would like to know more about *SOMA*, about going on a team, about giving to the work or about the vital work of intercessory prayer then please write, email or phone us at the following address:

*SOMA UK*

**PO Box 6002**
**Heath & Reach, Leighton Buzzard**
**Bedfordshire LU7 OZA**

*Going home*

# Introduction

*Cry For Sudan* has come out of a longing to see more people experiencing the heart-cry of this beautiful country. It is an appeal to be crying out to God to see powerful and lasting transformations of individual lives, churches and communities.

*SOMA* (Sharing of Ministries Abroad) has conducted many missions to The Episcopal Church of Sudan (ECS) at the invitation of local bishops. These have come out of a deep concern to help re-establish Christian life-style and community after the ravages of virtually forty years of civil war.

The specific inspiration for this book came out of two *SOMA* missions —to Kajo-Keji Diocese and Yei Diocese in 2003 and 2004. The idea first came while sharing a *tukel* – a round Sudanese grass roof hut – with Charles Laku, who is a huge enthusiast with a dynamic personality and a great sense of humour. We have shared in some memorable missions together. Charles is also a fearless evangelist and was the first of the clergy to return to his Kajo-Keji Diocese in southern Sudan during the war. Among other ventures, he was headmaster of a bombed out school.

It was June 2003, and I was part of the small team from the UK and Uganda that had caught the ferry over the huge River Nile and crossed the border into southern Sudan. The *SOMA* team were heading for the war-torn area of Kajo-Keji to bring leadership training about the work of the Holy Spirit in the Christian church today.

We spent ten days there and fanned out on the two Sundays to preach and take services in many villages and

*Delegates at Kajo-Keji, 2003*

nearby. Under the leadership of Don Brewin, the team was bringing teaching and leadership training on 'Living as a Prophetic Community'. About a hundred men and women came for the seminars and workshops, many of them walking huge distances to be present.

There was an uneasy ceasefire in place and our *SOMA* team was ten miles from the front lines. Charles and many others shared their heartaches, their pains, their stories of exile and their prayers for peace. All of us as team members were profoundly moved by what we saw and shared. So this is an attempt to convey such impressions through poetry, drawings and articles done at the time, at odd moments —sometimes late at night, by candlelight. The ideas are scattered and diverse and written in different styles. There is focus on love, on the beauty of the land, on the devastations of war, on deliverance ministry and on desperate longings.

A year later I had the privilege of leading a *SOMA* team to Yei Diocese, about 130 miles north-west, at the invitation of Bishop Hilary Luate Adeba. He asked us to give teaching for 170 of his clergy and leaders on the theme 'Created in Christ to do Good Works'. We were deeply touched by his leadership gifts and passion for Jesus. Again there were moments of scribbling down ideas and reaching for paints and paper.

Yei was the first diocese in southern Sudan to receive a *SOMA* team in November 1997, shortly after the liberation of the town by the SPLA (Sudan People's Liberation Army). This came at the invitation of the former bishop, The Right Reverend Seme Solomona, so a team, led by Don Brewin, came to give teaching on 'Discerning the Spirit in the Midst of Chaos'. Other bishops heard about this and, after discussions at the 1998 Lambeth Conference, a plan was agreed to continue the teaching for delegates from seven further dioceses: Ezo, Ibba, Lui, Maridi, Mundri, Rokon and Yambio. There was also much blessing through collaborative work with CMS (the Church Mission Society).

Two other bishops also feature in this book. Bishop Bullen Dolli, from Lui Diocese shares his experience of the power of prayer and forgiveness, and Bishop Manasseh Dawidi of Kajo-Keji Diocese relates remarkable stories of people raised from the dead.

Most southern Sudanese have grown up with war and the horrors of becoming refugees. It is thought that as many as eight million were forced into exile or joined the estimated four million Internally Displaced Peoples (IDPs). They have known civil war since the mid-1950s, when the predominantly black Christian population in the south rose up against the alienating policies of forced Islamisation and Arabisation by the mainly northern Arab government in Khartoum.

Despite the 2004 peace talks (in Naivasha, Kenya), Sudan remains deeply unsettled. The 2004 Darfur crisis in north-western Sudan resulted in what the United Nations described as 'the worst humanitarian crisis in the world'. In this case the largely Islamic Darfur population stood against the dehumanizing policies of the Khartoum government resulting in 1.5 million people being displaced in a struggle that has known no ethics. A further 50,000 were reported killed and 200,000 fled to refugee camps in Chad. There were many parallels to the root causes of civil war in the south.

The Sudan Council of Churches took a strong stand in September 2004, expressing deep concern that peace efforts were going so slowly and that such brutal warfare was still taking place in different parts of the country. The Anglican Communion News Service reported on the Council's worries that the government seemed increasingly bent on further war, and incitement of violence, rather than peace.

At the same time, famine struck Kajo-Keji, with people driven to eating leaves. Food stocks gave out due to an unexpected early return of exiles from the Uganda refugee camp of Adjumani. This came about because soldiers from the so-called Lord's Resistance Army (LRA) attacked Adjumani, forcing refugees to flee back to Kajo-Keji, resulting in the famine. Many believe the attack was orchestrated by the Sudan Government, which gives funding and military aid to the LRA, as a deliberate ploy to foment unrest and starvation.

It was in Kajo-Keji, just a year earlier, that I had shared a grass-roofed *tukel* with Charles. Then, as the early morning sunlight streamed in the tiny window, I told him of my thoughts about a possible book. His encouragement was characteristically direct: "Well, you'd better get on with it," he said from behind his mosquito net. "Because if God is telling you to do it, He wants it to happen!"

So thank you Charles, Bishops Hilary, Bullen and Manasseh and also Don Brewin and many others for your encouragement, example and prayers. Particular thanks to Rose Marie Edwards for your prayerful discernment in proof-reading. Most importantly, thank you to Libby – my wife – for all your love, long-suffering and patience when I get carried away by yet another enthusiasm!

My longing is that this book may be used for meditation and prayer, and encourage many more of us to 'cry for Sudan' in prayer and action. Perhaps, too, we will find ourselves crying out for other parts of our war-torn world, knowing that God can do far more than we can ever ask or think.

William Mather
Associate Director, *SOMA* UK
*November 2004*

*Path to 'Tukel Village', Kajo-Keji*

*Early morning at 'Tukel Village'*

*Ladies from Kajo-Keji move in worship as they experience the living water of Jesus*

# How to Use the
# Sketches and Poems

This book was born out of a desire to share thoughts and insights about southern Sudan that were originally expressed in paintings and poetry. These were put together in a smaller booklet in time for the *SOMA* Silver Jubilee Conference at Canterbury in July 2004. Afterwards, ideas developed for additional work, based on diaries kept at the time.

At the same time the paintings and poetry remain for me a significant *cri de coeur* that form the heart of this volume. The original paintings are mainly pen and watercolour and were, of course, in colour, though they can only be reproduced in this edition in monochrome form.

I have always loved to paint, so sketching kit inevitably crowds up my luggage. In this case the paintings and poems were all done separately and not intended to try and illustrate each other. However, they complement each other and the text so can be considered either together or separately according to personal preference. The paintings and drawings are all done very quickly, for that is my style and in most cases there was no time for anything else. Sometimes they happen bouncing around in a bus or car. The result is often quite sketchy. What is of personal value is whether they have integrity. It is whether such images reflect back again those vital moments of the numinous; of Holy Spirit prompting and awareness.

In this sense they are for me an activity of prayer rendered visual and, as such, are hopefully of value and inspiration to others. The frontiers between painting and prayer can become very blurred. At best, such paintings can become an aid to contemplation.

What I would like to suggest is using these for your personal meditation and prayer. It may help to sit quietly somewhere, away from distraction. A poem, or a section of a poem, can then be read, and time given to think about it prayerfully.

Similarly, take a look at a painting. Imagine yourself in the situation. Watch the people. See them walking, dancing, talking, learning. See their joys and their heart-aches and pains. Look out across the landscapes, so beautiful and so devoid of so-called modern trappings. Be aware of the devastations of war, and pray for the land and the people. Let the Holy Spirit guide you, as you do so, into further realms of spiritual awareness.

Give yourself time to do this. You may find that deep emotions start welling up; that tears begin to flow; that unexpected feelings of anger emerge. Often, what is happening is that you are entering into the compassion of our heavenly Father, and His hatred of the sin which causes such cruel suffering. Turn such feelings into prayer. There may be a sense of outrage, of criticism. This is quite normal and, in fact, a healthy sign that you are feeling the burden of pain. If so, again turn it into prayer. Too many people misunderstand this and retreat into criticism.

I believe that in such moments God would not have us run from such thoughts and feelings. Allow them space and soil in your own emotions. For as you do so, so you are sharing God's heart. You are entering into His grieving and compassion for those situations and people. And as you are open to His promptings in this realm of spiritual awareness, so the Holy Spirit will guide you, and will begin to bring about change in those areas you long for so much. Be encouraged; your prayers help turn the tide.

*Carrying the washing home from the well in Yei*

# Pilgrim Love

We are a pilgrim people
Who travel with nothing but love
We may carry other things
But the first is love
The love of Jesus in our hearts
Love for people who are different
Different personalities
Different sense of humour
Different priorities
Different perspectives
Different motivation
Different religion
Different background
We love because
He first loved us
And calls us to do likewise

*Yei: the detritus of war*

# War Zone

War zone. The front line is twelve miles away. On arrival in Kajo-Keji the team is startled by nearby violent explosions of heavy weapons, 'To test they are still working'. Landmines have left rusting remains of vehicles in ditches, half buried in the rainy season's new green grass.

Someone greets the team, "Things are safe now: there are no lootings, no rapes and no unnecessary killings."

All stone or brick-built buildings are pockmarked, roofless and most just piles of rubble with a few jagged pieces of masonry standing in the bright sunshine. Churches have been destroyed by the government soldiers 'from the north'. Four stone pillars are all that is visible of the church built by the missionaries at Romoggi. The rest is overgrown.

"In the dry season, the wild fires come," says Bishop Manasseh Dawidi. But so many people have fled, there is nobody to put them out, so the fires rampage on, taking with them grass-roofed *tukels* (houses) and churches.

After almost forty years of war, all the infrastructure of

the country is destroyed. A few hospitals remain, but even they are targets, to prevent injured soldiers being cared for and healed. In 2003 there were only twelve kilometres of tarmac roads, no electricity, no running water, no new investments, no large buildings, no tractors in the fields — in fact, very few visible fields. By the roads, occasional skull and crossbones signs warn of landmines. There are stories of children killed and maimed. A boy in hospital had lost three fingers playing with an army bullet. He was banging it on a stone.

There are long faces as you talk about the war, about the persecution as the Arabs overran the villages and towns, about the bravery of individuals, about the families fleeing to the bush and walking miles and miles to exile in Uganda and Kenya. Figures are hazy — possibly up to eight million in neighbouring countries, longing to return. Or the 'lost boys', some of whom have somehow ended up in the USA.

In the refugee settlements, schools have sprung up. There is even a theological college in a Ugandan camp, training clergy for future ministry back home. Houses have been built. Basic subsistence is just possible through farming of 'gardens' and creating home workshops. But families have been split, and many have grown larger as orphaned children have become dependants.

All that remains in the country which they have left is

the paradox of beauty and hope. The scars of war are being overgrown, the bomb craters are disappearing, the rusting, useless lorries on their sides are being pillaged for housing materials and cooking pots. Corrugated iron roofs of schools stolen by the government soldiers for their bunkers are being replaced. The countryside is beautiful and appears unspoilt. Inside the classrooms there are piles of rubble and, in Kajo-Keji, faint wall paintings by children obsessed with war and expressing their feelings in crude graffiti of people carrying guns or kneeling in surrender. At the orphanage in Adjumani refugee settlement, a teenager had an arm severed below the elbow. He had been found like that as a baby.

In the centre of it all is the church —unbelievably vibrant and alive. Today they face different problems. One priest said that when the persecutions came his congregation scattered. Now new churches were emerging as 'preaching posts' under mango trees. "How do we help them grow?" he asked. Work is also being done to ensure good relationships with other denominational groups, such as Roman Catholics and Pentecostals.

The pain of the past is excruciating. So many have been killed or maimed, or driven from home. But people are coming back. They are beginning to return, and they know their own plots of land and where the church sites used to be. In Kajo-Keji, the church faces the challenge of proper surveying to ensure they have title to their land. There is the challenge of encouraging new investment in building materials, of a new home for the bishop and senior clergy, and of a truck for transporting materials for homes and agriculture. There are dilemmas such as whether to invest in a tractor or teams of oxen for ploughing. It is not just the machines themselves, but how to maintain and service them in a land of few spare parts. A further dilemma for the church in the war zone is what can be begun now and what must wait.

There is a weariness over war, and longing for peace. This can only be achieved by Christians and Muslims, black Africans and Arabs talking together and reaching some kind of agreement. While we were there, the peace negotiators in Kenya were working hard to achieve this. Their efforts will only bear fruit with major international pressure, perseverance and publicity. For after so many years of war, the feelings go deep and now, with the discovery of oil, there are other and more complicated vested interests of greed at play.

The history is littered with broken peace agreements. The Christians say they want peace, forgiveness, reconciliation and to find a compromise. They complain that the Arabs in the north want no such thing, and that such words do not belong to their language or teachings. They find it hard to trust Islamic negotiators, for so often they have broken their word or treaty. In the meantime the southern

Christian army – the Sudan People's Liberation Army (SPLA) – pushed the Islamic government forces back. At the front line the two armies faced each other in an uneasy ceasefire as the politicians talked.

The debate continues over whether there can be a 'united' Sudan or whether the future is for an Islamic Arab state in the north and a Christian black south, each entering a new phase of freedom to govern themselves, live and worship.

Christians are praying for forgiveness to break the terrible cycle of revenge. Even secular statesmen like the Kajo-Keji District Commissioner are saying that love is the most important thing.

After forty years of war, there must be a better way.

*Yei town*

# A Beautiful Epitome of Suffering

The waitress looked barely out of her teens. She was pretty, with a beautiful smile but an indefinable air of sadness. She was a Sudanese refugee.

The team had spent the whole previous day driving the ninety miles from Yei on the incredibly bumpy red-dust road into Uganda. A cheap hotel was found, and it was there that we encountered this beautiful young life who seemed in so many ways to epitomise the sufferings of Sudan. We identified with her very quickly. It turned out her family had come from Yei and they still have a plot of land behind the hospital. Her father was from Yei and her mother from Kajo-Keji. She told us that her father was killed in the war and her family had fled. They reached a refugee camp in Uganda. Her mother contracted a serious illness in the camp but there was no medicine to treat her. She died nine months later. One of her brothers also died there.

Not surprisingly for a woman so beautiful, she married very young and quickly had two children. Shortly afterwards her husband died, leaving her a widow at the age of twenty. Now she has another man but he treats her badly and goes with other women. Because of the war and accompanying troubles, she had had to give up her education. Now, she desperately wants to earn more money for her children. She also wants to be able to do some kind of course of study for future work when she can leave exile and go back home. Somehow she seemed to exemplify the best and worst of Sudan. She has seen more suffering, outrage and desolation than most Westerners could possibly imagine, let alone experience. Despite everything she has a radiant faith in Christ, and almost her first words were: "I am a born again Christian." She asked the team to pray for her, which we did with tears in our eyes. Despite the unlikely venue – sitting round a plastic-topped table in the dining room, with a television blaring nearby – the presence of God was real and powerful.

It was agonising not to be able to do more. Next day we had to leave and spent three hours sitting beside a grass airstrip, hoping and praying that an unscheduled plane would arrive to take us to Kampala. There, by the grace of God, while sipping cold drinks in a tiny café, we bumped into the pastor of a local church, and he promised to see what he and his church could do to help the waitress.

A tiny, twelve seat plane finally did arrive. It was empty and going to Kampala, and if we had tickets we could climb aboard. Gratefully, we did so, and took off with the yellow bush grasses tearing away beneath the undercarriage. Quickly, we rose above the dark green mango trees and into a pale blue sky, leaving behind experiences of much joy and desperate suffering. Catching this plane was itself one among many minor miracles that we had been privileged to share over the previous two weeks of mission. Now there were tears of sadness at coming to the end of such a fruitful time. There was also a deep sense of thankfulness that there was at least some hope for our new-found waitress friend.

*Main runway, Arua airport*

# So Little, So Much

A suffering people
So much pain
So much agony
So many families split up
So many congregations scattered
So many still in exile
So many longing for peace
So many visions and dreams
So many hopes
So few people here
So few materials
So much to be done
So little money — yet
So much faith
So much love

*Cyclist, Yei*

# We Need Total Renewal

During March 2004 a *SOMA* team visited Yei in southern Sudan. Before the mission I had had a remarkable opportunity in the UK of meeting Bishop Hilary Luate Adeba, who outlined the needs of the diocese. He had just been appointed bishop and was in London at the invitation of Lambeth Palace for special training. He was taking over from the much-loved bishop, The Right Reverend Seme Solomona, who had died. Bishop Hilary shared his own heartaches and longings. Ironically, four months later he was refused a visa by the British High Commission in Uganda when he applied to come to the UK for the *SOMA* Silver Jubilee Conference in Canterbury.

In the incongruous setting of Heathrow Airport departure lounge, Bishop Hilary said, "The diocese has almost died. There have been no activities, direction or guidance since the old bishop became ill in 1996.

"My coming to the diocese means we have got to seek a vision of renewal for the people of Yei in the diocese. This is a renewal that is spiritual, that will bring a good system of governing and administration, a strong development system, and will improve education and health systems.

"We need total renewal. There needs to be training of people, evangelists, pastors. We also need to target the youth and the women. It is complete renewal that is needed. When you come with a *SOMA* team we need you to come and begin a process of renewal for the diocese. We alone can't do it. We need support from *SOMA*. I want your team to help us make a step to initiate renewal and hope for the people of Yei. We need to start everything anew.

"We are struggling. It is a struggle. We need a strong faith in Jesus so we can do the work. There are so many challenges. We need to get ourselves right. I know when the *SOMA* team comes, I know the renewal will come.

"I was there last year at the bishops' retreat in Kampala with *SOMA* —that's how I know that it was important to have *SOMA* to come to the diocese. The idea of renewal is very serious in my mind. We need you to help us exercise compassion and give hope."

After the mission, Bishop Hilary wrote: "I am writing to express our profound gratitude for the *SOMA* team…we feel blessed for the tremendous moments of sharing in a deeper way the good news of our Lord Jesus Christ. Over 170 people came to the conference and we hope to see the impact…on our church workers in time to come. It has been great to see the Holy Spirit of God moving among us and opening us up for repentance and forgiveness. During a moving sermon…in the Cathedral Church of Emmanuel, Yei, lots of people accepted Jesus as their Saviour. I am deeply touched…at a time when we are praying for renewal after a disturbing history in our diocese for many years."

## Obstacles to 'Cleansing the Land'

Many, like Bishop Hilary, long for a deep spiritual cleansing of their land, but there are major obstacles. You could say that the people of southern Sudan have every reason to be angry about the harsh regimes and ideologies that have tried to rule their country for so long. For forty years such things have brought only war, bloodshed and the breakdown of trust.

When challenged to think about some of the things that prevent such transformation taking place, the clergy of Yei were able to think on a bigger scale than just blaming the war. Although the war clearly shapes much of their thinking, here are some of the perceptions that were shared in a public meeting:

1. Anger: there is anger because of wrong things that have been done; there is anger over looting during the war and many find it difficult to forgive.

2. Children: during the war many never went to school and there is a whole generation of young adults who have missed

out on education. For others, the school fees required for any school are too high.

3. Loss of leadership and many good people because of the war.

4. Destruction of most buildings and property because of the war.

5. People dying of Aids.

6. Many people deciding not to come to church.

7. People not listening to church leaders.

8. Clergy children not behaving as well as they should.

9. Tribalism.

10. Injustice: a system of justice hardly exists.

11. Need for reconciliation with one group of churches that has separated from the diocese.

12. Christians still seeing witch doctors.

13. A plague of grasshoppers destroying crops this year.

14. The need to care for orphans and feed them.

15. Anger towards Arab people.

16. Hatred developing between small communities, often caused by small misunderstandings.

17. Disunity in families where some are Christians and some not.

18. People telling lies about other people.

19. Lack of forgiveness.

20. The extra burdens placed on women in families where the husband has been killed in the war. Many women weep

a great deal because the responsibilities are so hard.

21. Demonic interference in people's lives.

22. Exiles who return believing they have found new magic and ideas in other religions or from witch doctors.

23. Problems when young people get married and the dowry is not paid.

24. Children being hurt because of the war.

25. Reaching out with the Christian gospel to new areas is so hard because of poor roads and communication systems.


For the church leaders in Yei this simple exercise of listing so many problems was a major step forward in itself. It became clear that here was a framework for intercessory prayer and for personal prayer ministry, towards the goal of seeing their people and their communities truly converted and transformed.

Such insights come out of the awareness of the power of prayer to change things. As a tool for change such intercessory prayer is powerful, but homework is needed. There is a need for practical research into an area to find out what are the real problems. Some describe this as making a spiritual map onto which all the needs and problems — both physical and spiritual — can be drawn. In prayer this can be used by intercessors to navigate around the area to help usher in healing, forgiveness and cleansing.

This then becomes part of the process of welcoming the

power of Jesus Christ into an area, so it is made clean and transformed. With such prayer there can be fresh support, encouragement and vision for the very practical tasks that so many are called to in the creation of churches, communities and countries.

## Flying in the Spirit

As people begin to experience the Holy Spirit in their lives, so a greater openness to God develops —and so healings begin to happen. In Yei, many stories were shared, all testifying to the Holy Spirit working in people's lives. For many, the ministry in groups was a real surprise and miracle. It was emphasized this was a sovereign work of God and not in any way manipulated.

People opened their hearts and lives to Him, building confidence after much teaching and ministry, particularly about repentance and forgiveness. Consequently, the Holy Spirit was able to reach deep down, highlighting areas such as sin, sickness, anger and unforgiveness. In His strength, with an awareness of the mighty love of God, so deep inner and physical healing began to take place.

For the team, this breakthrough began to take place as we abandoned our set programme and allowed the Holy Spirit to show us His. This led into a time of the team repenting of sin, opening up to God and to each other. Then, as we called out in prayer, often with much weeping, so He showed us His way and gave us His vision. During this time there was a real gift of faith that if the team were able to provide a demonstration of how to pray for somebody who was sick, this would be a key to unlocking more effective ministry.

A CMS worker, Billy Smyth, had asked us, the day before, "Have you experienced some kind of breakthrough?" We had to admit ruefully that we had not. There had been a lot of repentance, but no major times of ministering in the power of the Holy Spirit. That following morning, the team were all longing to see a more obvious breakthrough. There were many encouragements but we were not 'there' yet. We were also feeling a bit guilty for sometimes stopping the flow of the Holy Spirit in a meeting, because we had come to 'the end' of our official meeting time. All of us were concerned and passionate to see more. We started discussing how best to go forward until somebody suggested praying about it all, first and foremost. So we prayed. There followed a long time of prayer, during which we sensed the Lord saying: 'Start as you mean to go on; go for the main thing first; don't leave it till last.' This was the key. The team felt we should start with our Uganda team member, Margaret Kiswiriri, teaching on 'Prayer and Power'. We then agreed to move into a time of demonstrating how to pray for the sick in the power of the Holy Spirit. After that, we would simply have to trust the Lord for any teaching that had to be left out of our 'programme'.

In the end we did not reach a point of actually doing the demonstration until after our 11.00 a.m. tea break. But it was still the key; the breakthrough. This was the moment of storming the apparently impregnable strongholds before us. It was as if the Holy Spirit showed us the way and provided the ladders with which to clamber over the barricades. The result was an almost tangible perception of Satan being defeated yet again, and of some wonderful victories for Jesus as He blessed the church leaders and gave them deep inner healing. In turn, there was confidence that they would be able to go back to their churches to share the teaching they had experienced, not just out of head knowledge, but because they had personally experienced the presence and power of the living God. The fruit of it all was much happiness, joy and peace, with effortless dancing, and glorifying Jesus as we all jigged around in a big dusty circle under the mango trees.

The final session ended with fun as Felicity had brought her kite. Felicity Angus (now Leakey) was at one point a missionary in Rwanda, until forced to leave in the terrible 1984 genocide when over a million people were killed. She has seen many different aspects of Christian ministry. For now it was the ministry of the kite. It was a frameless kite with air vents to give lift, and came complete with the smiling face of Thomas the Tank Engine emblazoned on it. Nothing could be more inappropriate than Thomas the

Tank Engine in a community with no railways, no proper roads, no industry and no children's books. But Thomas was a star. He rose into the air magnificently, reaching higher even than the huge spreading mango trees which had served us so well with shade and shelter in the searing heat of the day. Up he went, to great interest from the ground.

There was also some interest from the sky. He was quickly spotted by some real kites, soaring on the thermals as tiny specks, a considerable distance above. Down they stooped with a rush, thinking this was lunch, only to be outwitted by a terrific loop from Thomas. Everyone on the ground applauded, and the embarrassed kites swirled away over the trees. There was much laughter and humour but Thomas, like the Fool in King Lear, also had a more subtle message. It was as if the kite is each one of us, and that as we allow ourselves to be filled with the wind of the Spirit so we can fly high above our normal expectations, and so we can overcome surprise attacks from unwelcome quarters. Also, it was clear that the kite needed somebody firm on the ground to hold the string so it could fly. This became a further message of the need to be firmly standing – or rooted – with Christ to see such flight and effectiveness in our lives taking place. So thank you, Thomas; thank you, Sudan; and thank you, Lord.

# Under the Mango Trees

*Under the mango trees in Yei: workmen resting*

Sun setting in the compound
Sounds of young people singing
Under the mango trees
Guitar and simple stringed instruments
Gentleness, simplicity, love
Childlike love reaching up to the Father

Intimacy in worship
A quality lacking so often
In grown-ups
Hardened
By war
By anger
By hurts
By disappointments
By soldiers who have
Killed family members
By unjust systems
By looting of personal property
By raping of women
By destroying homes, families
Villages and towns
By laying mines
Even in the bishop's garden
By littering the ground with bullets
For children to pick up
By bitterness born of war
By orphans who can't be looked after
By mothers who despair
Of being able to care for children
Because father has been killed
And she's alone
With her own children and

The orphaned children of
Relatives who have died in war
Or through the increasing
Scourge of Aids

So the adults move
Slowly into forgiveness
In solemn silence
Repenting of attitudes that
Have blocked up flows of love
That have prevented
Holy Spirit freedom
To flood their beings
Bringing gifts and fruit for
Life and ministry

Slowly they come
Slowly they open up
Slowly the tears come to eyes
Slowly they realise
They can experience release
From the horrors that
Have stifled so long
That have spread further
Misunderstanding, hurts
And hate

Slowly forgiveness of enemies
Is coming
Slowly but in a way
That is real and special
And precious
Gentle, undemonstrative
But real
A matter of the heart
That can be lovingly
Encouraged and developed
Then will come the releasing
And the blessing and
The filling with Holy Spirit
Joy and peace
Supernatural fruit and gifts
For the building of
The 'New Sudan'

And so the young people
Sing in their artless
And simple way
There are tears in adult eyes
For they are receiving already
And bringing hope

*Under the mango trees:
the secondhand clothes market in Yei*

*Carrying heavy loads of wood in Yei*

# Let Love Prevail

Love the sustaining  principle
Hard days ahead
Forty years
Of war behind
A land scattered
And bruised
By hatred, bloodshed
Religious fanaticism
Desires for domination.
Time for change
There can be no more
War zones
No more deaths of innocents
There must be talks
Inspired by love
Recognised by Christian
And Muslim leaders alike.

There can be no more
Manipulation
Coercion by fear.
It is the quality of love
Prepared to repent, forgive
And reconcile that is
So desperately needed.
We cannot continue
Hating those who are different
We must love them as people
Made in the image of God
Pray for them
Pray for God to bless them
And pray that
In the peace
The love of Jesus will prevail
And move mountains
That the exiles may return
That the land may be tilled
That there may be further
Mushrooming of *tukels*
As families are reunited
And homes are built in the
Former killing fields
Of devastation

*Ladies in Yei fetch fresh water from the well*

# No Sounds of Traffic

Bustling Kampala,
Motorbikes, traffic, smells
Noise, hooters, buses
Birds singing
All the activity
And enterprise
Of a city that is alive
And free from war

A far cry from Yei
With its solitude
Its quiet
The only early-morning sound
The drums
In a distant village
Or the low murmur
Of voices

As people walk barefoot
Along the dusty road
Or the mid-morning
Laughter of children
Sitting on the ground outside
The grass-roofed school
Or the simple sounds
Of people
Washing or preparing food

Occasionally but only
Very occasionally
There is the roar of a
Huge African lorry
Towing an enormous trailer
Piled high with produce
Lashed together with rope
Bulging in all directions
Covered in red dust
And a few people
Clinging on top

A food delivery has made it
From Uganda or the Congo
All stop and wave
At this engineering miracle

From another world
Bringing vital supplies
For survival

For that is what it is
Survival
Where there is no electricity
No running water
No telephones
No tarmac roads
Life is survival

And still the ravages of war
Hang close
The twisted metal wrecks
That once were cars
Or lorries
Now rusting in the dust
And long grass
The pock-marked ruins of
The few brick buildings
The craters
The absence of animals
And the memories that
Leave invisible scars
Of killings, of rape

Of wounding
Of families destroyed
Separated, exiled
Of education ruined
Some with no schooling
For twenty years

Yet things are slowly
Recovering
Exiles returning "to look"
Before they bring
Their families
*Tukels* being built
Bricks being fired
Former Arab prisoners-of-war
Now freed
And selling produce
In the bustling market

There is a buoyancy
And a hope
But deep wariness and
Suspicion of
Government motives
In the peace talks

Only international intervention
Can secure
A lasting peace
With treaties that will hold
And until peace
There can be no
Major developments
No big investments
No major new road projects
No big shops
No factories

It is stalemate time
Longing for peace
But not there yet
It could all turn sour
So quickly
The fighting could all
Begin again
As in Darfur

There is willingness
And determination to fight
But after forty years of war
Both sides are tired
Of battle

They want peace
They long for the day
When there will be
The bustle and noise
And smells
And inconvenience
Of traffic

*In the market at Yei which in this area is hot, cramped,
busy, colourful with people and where some of the traders
are former Arab prisoners-of-war who on release have
decided to settle in Yei*

*Woman with baby*

# The Power of Prayer and Forgiveness

Moses, a church leader in Yei, explained how many people found it almost impossible to forgive atrocities they had witnessed. He himself had seen a church full of praying Christians burned to the ground by government soldiers, and everybody in it killed. In addition, he had seen his own church torched and his home and property destroyed. Although nobody was killed, his wife was abducted by the soldiers and he did not see her for three months.

It was only when he began to experience healing prayer through the *SOMA* team visit that he came to a place of being able to forgive the perpetrators. He said that as two other people prayed for the Holy Spirit to touch him and bless him he felt overwhelmed by waves of God's love. It was at that point, he was able to testify later, that he came to a new place of being able to forgive.

Others had similar stories. Bishop Bullen Dolli of Lui Diocese was able to share his own experience of the power of forgiveness and prayer. Speaking to a *SOMA* Prayer

Conference in the UK in 2003, he used the analogy of the prophet Daniel, who 'prayed three times a day and God saved him from the lions'.

Speaking at the Wycliffe Bible Centre, near High Wycombe, he said we must do likewise. "We must pray without ceasing, when driving, working in the garden, cooking and so on. Pray, so you do not enter into temptation." He then added simply that prayer is like a telephone to heaven, and the telephone line is a combination of both, "our faith and our fasting". He then startled everyone by asking, "Have any of you seen somebody killed in your church?" He told how, before he became bishop, a Lay Reader[1] was shot by government soldiers for praising God. They came into the church to tell the Christians to stop worshipping Jesus and be quiet. The Lay Reader refused to comply, and was shot dead with eight bullets through the brain. They left his body on the communion table as an example.

Dolli told his people that there should be no revenge for such acts – only forgiveness – otherwise the vicious circle would continue. A few weeks later he was in a church that was invaded by Islamic soldiers. They selected him and four others and marched them outside. It was about 9.00 a.m., and they gave them shovels to dig their graves. By 2.00 p.m. the holes were deep enough. They stood them at the end of the graves ready to shoot them. They tied blindfolds

[1] An Anglican church member licensed for preaching and pastoral work

on them, but Dolli refused to have a blindfold. He said, "I am only going to die once, and I want to see what is going on."

The captain agreed, and a soldier with a loaded gun stood in front of each man. Dolli then asked if, as a final request, he could say a prayer. The soldiers taunted him, saying, "Can your Jesus save you?" But they let him pray.

He thought about Jesus, and how on the cross He prayed for those who were murdering Him: "Father, forgive them, for they know not what they are doing."

So Dolli prayed, "Father I am ready to die. But please forgive these men for what they are about to do." He prayed in Arabic, which was their language.

As he prayed, something happened to the captain. He fell to the ground and dropped his pistol. He then called out: "Your God is alive!" The bishop believed this was a direct result of the Holy Spirit coming on the man and convicting him of the wrong he was about to do. The captain then ordered his men to remove the blindfolds from the others and set them free.

They returned to church, where the congregation were weeping and praying. This turned into much rejoicing, and they all sang together: 'Onward, Christian soldiers....' The bishop said this demonstrated both the power of prayer and the power of forgiveness.

He was tested still further when, shortly afterwards, soldiers murdered his brother. This happened because somebody falsely accused him of doing something that he had never done. The soldiers captured him. They put a rope round his neck and dragged him for three miles behind an army jeep. He quickly died, but the body swung from side to side on the road and most of the skin was removed. They then poured petrol over the body and burnt it to ashes. Despite all this, Bullen continued to insist that the only way forward was to keep practising the forgiveness of Jesus Christ. So he preached that he had forgiven the soldiers for murdering his brother. After preaching on one such occasion, somebody came up to him in the vestry afterwards and asked to speak to him. The man was asking for forgiveness. He explained, "I am the man who falsely accused your brother and caused his death. I am really sorry. I know I have done wrong and have deeply hurt you. I don't deserve this. But can you forgive me?"

For a moment Bullen looked at him gravely, before finally giving him a big hug and saying, "I forgive you." He then invited the man for a meal next day with his wife, at their home. Some delicious food was prepared, but to make absolutely clear there was no poison anywhere, Bullen insisted that they all ate from the same plate.

Furthermore, when his wife brought them some tea, he and the man both drank from the same large mug, and from exactly the same spot on the mug. This was to demonstrate that the friendship and forgiveness was real, and there was no revenge planned by placing poison on another part of the mug.

The man was overwhelmed by such an attitude. He became a committed Christian and is now a Lay Reader in the church.

"This," said Bishop Bullen Dolli, "is the power of prayer and the power of forgiveness."

*An impression of delegates at the 2003 Kajo-Keji SOMA teaching: here sitting in a school room, at children's desks*

# Desperate Longings in Eyes

People in need
Desperate longing in eyes
For sponsorship
For children's schooling
For further education
For hospital bills
For materials
For the school roof
For an agricultural
training centre
For rebuilding the
bishop's house
ruined in battles
For needs here
For needs there
And each a priority

Got to take them
one by one
Not say yes or no
But listen and pray
Wait and consult
And only then decide

*Carrying water from the borehole, Yei*

*Kajo–Keji Church: preparing for morning worship*

# A Normal Sudan Sunday

After a light breakfast, two of us leave by motorbike on twisting Sudanese red dust paths for the 10.00 a.m. service in the grass-roofed parish church. The service in Kajo-Keji old town lasts three hours, with a message on 'Forgiving Enemies', after which five people come forward for healing prayer.

Lunch afterwards at about 1.00 p.m. is under a corrugated iron shelter near a bombed-out building. At 2.00 p.m. we go to the local hospital to pray for TB patients, a number of children, a landmine casualty and several ladies. By 4.30 we join a lively praise march to the market, led by a lady Lay Reader with a megaphone —all are singing and dancing. By the time it comes to preach – again on the theme of forgiveness – there is a very receptive crowd. The Holy Spirit comes in power, bringing blessing and conviction. Four demons are cast out of a frenzied teenage girl. The crowd worship throughout, with singing, leaping and dancing. Market traders watch with interest. The sun goes down, in a blaze of glorious primary colour, as we return to the hospital to baptise two babies who are near death.

On leaving, we discover the bishop sitting disconsolate on a bench as his vehicle has broken down. He has been returning with *SOMA* team members from church services farther afield. At 8.00 p.m., in near darkness, we return by motor-bike to the school compound and organise a rescue vehicle. The day ends with a light supper of rice, cassava and tea as the team has a time of sharing and prayer under the Southern Cross. We bed down for the night in the comfort of our round grass huts, to the sound of cicadas and tree frogs in the cool of the night.

The end of a normal Sunday in southern Sudan.

*War and peace, Kajo-Keji, 2003*

# Freedom for a Teenager

There is a challenge and thrill to open-air preaching. This is particularly so where the needs are very obvious and where people are open and want to listen. In Kajo-Keji there was an opportunity to preach on Sunday afternoon in the market place. Only a year before, it had been deserted because of the war. Now the large, red dust square was surrounded by wooden market stalls, with the colourful bustle of trading.

Members of local churches had marched in a lively procession to the square and, once there, gave themselves to exuberant worship, joy and dancing. The worship created a wonderful awareness of the presence of God. It also opened up an opportunity for deliverance ministry to a young woman who was quite clearly afflicted by demon spirits.

This became a very special time of personal ministry. It is here related in almost note form, to condense the intensity of the experience and provide an opportunity for others to share in the lessons learned.

Extraordinary humbling privilege
Preaching in a crowded market square
With a megaphone
Sharing the gospel
With people all around responding openly

A deep stillness
Of attentiveness
Good news reaching out
And touching hearts
A deep seriousness of expression
Thoughtfulness and openness

The Holy Spirit present
In Word, praise, testimony and dancing
His presence convicting
A demonised teenager
Flailing around
In staring-eyed madness

Spirits had come in
To bring comfort in orphaned rejection
A false comfort on the wings of fear

# FREEDOM FOR A TEENAGER

Hurt and deep sadness
Parents gone and the spirits
Coming in surrogate authority
Now confronted by true spiritual power
Agitated, annoyed, displaying
Their own foolishness
Creating fascination and fear
In bystanders
Attempting to wrest power and authority
From the Christians
And lord it themselves

Deliverance, teaching and solitude needed
Keeping a clear focus on Jesus
Not on her
Help the crowd to pray and share
In understanding and authority
So victory is in its rightful place

Take her somewhere quiet
Talk to her gently
Guard her from the exhibitionism
Of violent movements
Writhing on the ground
Removing clothes

Keep her standing
Speak to her with dignity, love
And power
Assure her of trust
Eye-contact and authority

A team-work ministry
Women in equal partnership
So she is not surrounded by men
Children kept from the open door
Idle bystanders and curiosity seekers
Asked to move on

An open shop
Empty with no walls at front or back
Earthen floor and mud walls
Simple, effective and a semblance of solitude
Space to breathe from the excited crowd

Now time to minister
In gentleness and authority
To allow the spirits to speak
And name themselves

Four different spirits from
A mountainous area in Uganda

# FREEDOM FOR A TEENAGER

Speaking in that language
With men's voices from the girl
Saying they were looking after her
Since the traumas of being orphaned

False comforters pleading to stay
Now told to go again
Many attempts in the market
Had been resisted
Too much bustle, noise and distraction

Now in the relative peace of
God's presence in the empty shop
There is space to focus
To give dignity and assurance of love
Despite moments still of
Staring-eyed white-of-eyeball frenzy

But the command to go is sure
Despite the pleadings and attempts
To bargain for further residency rights

Arms go limp, tears flow
The rigidity is gone
Peace prayers flow
Penitence is present

A willingness to turn to Him
Who has brought the release and change
Allowing the true Spirit of Jesus to enter
And bring full control and peace

So commitment can take place
In a simple prayer of sanity

A quietness descends
A few more tears
Rolling down dusty cheeks
But all is well
The storm is gone
There is peace and contentment
A calmness and joy
Clothing is dusted down
A bright orange track-suit top
Is put back on

A young woman
Emerges, restored,
Smiling shyly
Talking normally
And leaves with friends
Feminine and free

*Postscript: The young woman has remained free, and made a personal commitment to follow Jesus Christ. She is now happily married.*

*Path through the grass, Yei*

# Creation's Response

Sketches as we travel
Brief pen impressions
Of southern Sudan
Of Kajo-Keji
Of driving to the border
Of crossing the Nile

Moments of visual intensity
Seeing and registering
Collages of fleeting images
Creating compositions
Of many passing ideas
Attempts at feeling and
Recording the pain
The beauty
The limitless horizons
The solitude

# CREATION'S RESPONSE

The emptiness caused
By war
Yet the astonishing
And glorious beauty
Of natural forms
As if all creation
Conspires together
To overgrow
The bomb craters
The rusting fragments
Of landmine blasted
Vehicles
The precarious rubble of
The few stone houses

For around and over them
Grow lank green grasses
Shooting upwards in
Luxuriant rainy season vigour
Broad-leafed teak trees
And massive mangos
Shed acres of shade for
Deep contemplation

All is growing and singing
And flowering
Bringing hope
In the wake of
Man's devastations

*At the borehole*

# Raised From the Dead

Despite having so little in material benefits, the faith of the Christians in southern Sudan is powerful, alive and has stood the tests of adversity and persecution. During the *SOMA* mission to his diocese, The Right Reverend Manasseh Dawidi, Bishop of Kajo-Keji Diocese, Sudan, shared some remarkable stories of lessons learned from people being raised from the dead. The bishop was asked in a private conversation whether he knew of any cases of people being raised from the dead. "Oh yes," he said, "there have been many, many." These are three of the examples he shared. When giving permission for these stories to be published here, he said: "It will be wonderful to have more people know about these stories and the way God has been working so powerfully here."

## Go Back and Start Giving

*Woman from Lugbara tribe from Madi, Western Nile, Uganda circa 1949/50.*

The woman died suddenly. She lived in a nice house in an area where the custom regarding burial was that the deceased would be buried outside the house. A man would be buried on the right of the door, a woman on the left.

She died one afternoon and the body was left all night and next day, until after the heat of the day. She was then carried for burial, wrapped in a shroud, lying on a bamboo mat. The grave was prepared and ready, and the mourners were weeping and wailing. Movement was seen in the shroud, so the body was unwrapped. The woman sat up and said, "What is going on here?" She then told how she had been taken to heaven. While there, she was shown her house, which was all bare.

She asked why this was, and was told: "It is bare because you are not giving anything to the church. You must go back and put this right." She came back and told many people this story in many different places.

## Go Back and Restore Relationships

*The Reverend Nicodemus Gillia Ngirima from Mundri, Sudan. Circa 1970. Bishop Manasseh had met him and heard this story from him.*

The Reverend Nicodemus died at quite a young age. He

had been ill for some time. There was terrible grieving by relatives as they carried him to the grave. As they prayed and prepared to bury him, they saw movement. He had been clearly dead, but was now alive. His graveclothes were removed.

He told how he went to heaven and saw somebody very beautiful. He was asked, "Who are you?"

He replied, "I am Nicodemus."

"What do you do?"

"I preach about the Lord Jesus Christ."

"Yes," the person replied. "We know about you."

Then he saw a vision of two elders in his church who were jealous of each other, and fighting. The person said, "You have done nothing to stop this fighting. If you do nothing you will die without mercy."

He was given two texts. The first was from Mark 1:15, "The kingdom of God is near. Repent and believe the good news!" [NIV] The second was from Acts 1:8, "You will receive power when the Holy Spirit comes on you; and you will be my witnesses in Jerusalem, and in all Judea and Samaria, and to the ends of the earth." [NIV]

He came back to earth with this message, starting in Sudan and then to Uganda, where the bishop met him. He preached repentance in the name of Jesus, starting where he was but, as time went by, reaching people and places farther away.

## Go Back and Share this Message

*Mr Panuel Laloka, from Kajo-Keji, southern Sudan. Circa 1980. Panuel was a nephew of Bishop Manasseh and a class 4 student at the Elementary School in Romoggi.*

In the June holidays, Panuel got leprosy. It came very fast and his fingers, lips, ears and eyes all swelled up. After two weeks his fingers started to come off. His lips became very thick. He became very worried and felt very unlucky. He kept asking, "Why should this happen to me?" He began thinking of suicide —either to strangle himself or drown himself in the river. He planned that, when the family woke up one day, he would pretend to be asleep and then sneak out of the house to the river and drown himself. But during the night he died. The bishop said, "The Lord Jesus came to him and pressed him down, and his spirit was taken."

He was then taken along a wide path from the earth to the sky. He saw a crowd of people —a huge crowd processing along a wide road. Some were on foot, some on bicycles, some in cars, others in planes. Some were well-dressed, some in rags. He decided to join the procession.

He met a fine young man who showed him a different road which was very narrow. He did not want it. He was lifted up by the man and asked him why he was showing such care and love to him, a leper. "I am Jesus," the man said. "Come this way."

There was a very beautiful table in a big building ahead.

On the table was a wonderful book, edged in gold. "Panuel," he said, "come here." The man opened the book from beginning to end. Then he closed it with a key.

A door opened and he saw Mary, the mother of Jesus, and many others. He was carried to the end of the building. There was another building. Many disciples came to him and carried him to the end of it. There were happy people in white. He was put down.

He opened a gate and went out. Something stopped him. The man asked, "Panuel, what do you see?"

Panuel replied, "I see a hole with smoke."

"Panuel, what do you hear?"

He replied, "I hear the noises of the voices of people: many people of the country."

The man said, "Did you see a long procession?"

"Yes."

"These people are the ones crying there." The man continued, "We heard that you wanted to commit suicide. We rescued you. If you had killed yourself you would be in the procession."

The angel Gabriel said to him, "We have brought you here to see all these things; to see the place of Mary and Peter. You can choose which way you prefer to live.

"Now go back to earth. Ignore the criticism from people about being leprous. Ignore drunkards and drunkenness. Go to live a faithful Christian life. Believe in Jesus, repent of your sins, live a holy life. Then you will return one day.

"Pass this message on to many people. Wherever you go, share this message."

Panuel returned to earth. His leprosy was not healed, but he faithfully shared what he believed God had revealed to him, until his death.

*Studies of people in Yei, near the cathedral*

# Beautiful Land

A land so beautiful
So fertile and fair
Fields and trees
Growing open and free
Like an English parkland —
But there are palm trees
And teak trees
With enormous leaves —
Hardly England —
And at night the air is
Full of the tinkle and rasp
Of crickets and cicadas
And the comic burping
Of tree frogs

Sitting in the open late at night
With a torch for light
And the Southern Cross
In the stars far above

Time to wind down after the day
To eat rice and salad
Cassava and stringy meat

Time with the team
Talking out the day's events
Laughter, joking and at times
Struggling with
Different languages and cultures
Others simply sitting
And thinking and listening to
Happy conversations around

*Getting ready for the conference. Kajo-Keji, 2003*

# Affirm and Go

*The experience of being on a SOMA team is very rich, with many deep and powerful shared experiences in service and mission. By the very nature of being 'short term' mission, a time comes to move on. It is helpful, before the final goodbyes, to spend time together, affirming one another, praying for each other and releasing each other. In a spiritual sense, it provides an opportunity to let go of each other in a prayerful and supporting manner, so all can move on in love. This poem is an attempt to encapsulate this.*

Affirmation of ministry
Sharing as a team for the last time
Praying for each other
One by one, but also
Randomly, spontaneously
Sitting around in a room

An order and structure
But freedom in the Spirit
Affirmed in the Spirit
Affirmed in love
Supported and prayed for

Deep prayers of appreciation
Respect, integrity
Insight and authority

A fitting farewell and
Disengagement from
Each other

For after the intensity
Of mission and ministry
It is now time to move on

# What Peace?

*Thoughts on the challenges to the Sudan,*
*if and when lasting peace comes.*

Death of the old
Promise of the new
How will we treat it?
Is this just another
Investment opportunity
When peace comes?
A challenge to
Western civilisation
A place where
Faith is already

Will peace mean blatant
Commercialism
Exploitation
Capitalism?
Or is there a

Better Way
That can bring beauty
From the ashes
And make Sudan
A healing voice
To the world?